CAN YOU IMAGINE?

by

Patricia McKissack

photographs by

Myles Pinkney

Richard C. Owen Publishers, Inc.
Katonah, New York

Meet the Author titles

Verna Aardema	*A Bookworm Who Hatched*	Jonathan London *Tell Me a Story*
Frank Asch	*One Man Show*	George Ella Lyon *A Wordful Child*
Eve Bunting	*Once Upon a Time*	Margaret Mahy *My Mysterious World*
Lois Ehlert	*Under My Nose*	Rafe Martin *A Storyteller's Story*
Jean Fritz	*Surprising Myself*	Patricia McKissack *Can You Imagine?*
Paul Goble	*Hau Kola Hello Friend*	Patricia Polacco *Firetalking*
Ruth Heller	*Fine Lines*	Laurence Pringle *Nature! Wild and Wonderful*
Lee Bennett Hopkins	*The Writing Bug*	Cynthia Rylant *Best Wishes*
James Howe	*Playing with Words*	Jean Van Leeuwen *Growing Ideas*
Johanna Hurwitz	*A Dream Come True*	Jane Yolen *A Letter from Phoenix Farm*
Karla Kuskin	*Thoughts, Pictures, and Words*	

Text copyright © 1997 by Patricia McKissack

Photographs copyright © 1997 by Myles Pinkney

Richard C. Owen Publishers, Inc.

PO Box 585

Katonah, New York 10536

Library of Congress Cataloging-in-Publication Data

McKissack , Pat , 1944-
    Can you imagine? / by Patricia McKissack ; photographs by Myles Pinkney .
    p . cm . - (Meet the author)
    Summary: The author of the Newbery Honor Book , "The Dark Thirty ," describes her life , how she became a writer , how her family helps with her writing , and how she gets her ideas .
    ISBN 1-878450-61-1
    1 . McKissack , Pat , 1944- –Biography–Juvenile literature .
2 . Afro-American women authors–20th century–Biography–Juvenile literature .
3 . Children's literature–Authorship–Juvenile literature . [1 . McKissack , Pat , 1944– .
2 . Authors , American . 3 . Afro-Americans–Biography . 4 . Women–Biography .]
I . Pinkney , Myles , illus. II .
Title . III . Series : Meet the author (Katonah , N.Y.)
PS3563.C38323Z464 1997
813' .54–dc21   96-37892

Editorial, Art, and Production Director *Janice Boland*

Production Assistant *Donna Parsons*

Color separations by Leo P. Callahan Inc., Binghamton, NY

Printed in the United States of America

9 8 7 6 5 4 3 2

To my family

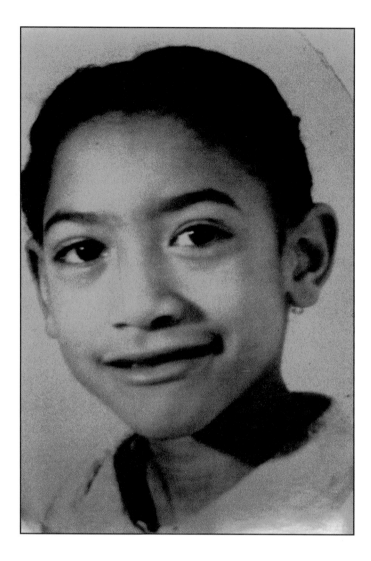

Dear Reader,

People often ask what helped me become a writer.

It was my imagination!

An early memory is of a field trip my class took
to a former president's house. Later we were asked
to tell a PTA group what we'd seen there.
I told about the mouse and rabbit who had shown
me around.

"You have a wonderful imagination,"
said my teacher, Mrs. Glore Ashford.
"It's a special gift. Use it."
And I have, all my life.

I was born in Smyrna,
Tennessee, August 9, 1944.
Shortly afterward,
my family moved to
St. Louis, Missouri.

I had two dogs, Buster and Smoky.
We went everywhere together.
I loved riding my bicycle and pretending
Buster and Smoky were my co-pilots.
We often went to the creek,
where I spent a lot of time *imagining*.

The summer of my tenth birthday, my parents divorced.
Mother moved us to Nashville, got a job, and rented
an apartment in the Preston-Taylor Housing Projects.
Daddy stayed in St. Louis.

My brother Nolan, my sister Sarah Frances,
and I visited him in the summer.

I had a loving family, good neighbors,
and encouraging teachers.
But the South of my childhood was often
cruel and unfair. It was segregated.
That meant black and white people could not
live, work, or go to school together.
The Nashville Library was not segregated.
It was one of the few public places
where I felt welcome.
Maybe that's why I loved reading.
I read everything, even the backs
of cereal boxes.
My favorite stories were world myths,
legends, and fairytales. They still are.
Sometimes when I'd finish a good book,
I'd use my imagination to make up
another ending for it, or a whole new story.

My Nashville grandparents had wonderful
imaginations, too. Nolan, Sarah, and I went to
Mama Frances's and Daddy James's house every
day after school to wait until our mother got off
from work.   Mama Frances told family stories.

Daddy James told stories about children with our
names. *Pat* in his stories could outsmart foxes
and catch the wind. Since this girl had my name,
I imagined I could do all the brave and wonderful
things she did.

It isn't hard to guess where I got the ideas for writing *Flossie and the Fox*,

Mirandy and Brother Wind, and *Nettie Jo's Friends*.

Other book ideas came from other storytellers
in my family. My St. Louis grandparents
were Mama Sarah and Papa Lucious.

Papa Lucious taught me to love music.
He hummed while he worked. When I'm writing
I hum music that goes with my words.
Mama Sarah told creepy, scary stories at twilight.

We kids called that time "The Dark Thirty,"
because we had thirty minutes to get home
before it got all the way dark and the monsters came out!

Many years later, I wrote *The Dark Thirty: Southern Tales of the Supernatural*. I dedicated my book to Mama Sarah. It was named a Newbery Honor Book in 1993. She was very proud.

When I learned how to write, I could really
let my imagination soar. All through grade school
and high school, I was forever scribbling a poem,
a play, or a story in a notebook.
English and Education were my majors in college.

After graduation from Tennessee State,
I married a classmate, Fredrick McKissack.

We moved to St. Louis in 1965, where our three sons, Fredrick, Jr. and the twins Robert and John, were born.

A few years later, I started teaching eighth grade English. There wasn't time to do much writing. But I kept a journal and wrote in it every day. I still keep one.

By 1971, I had completed my first book,
a biography of Paul Laurence Dunbar, my favorite
American poet. Dunbar interested me because
my mother recited his poetry. I had also jumped
rope to the rhythm of his poems.

Whenever I hear "Little Brown Baby,"
I remember our special time together,
just Mother and me.

I wanted my students to know Dunbar's work.
Since there was no children's biography about him
in the library, I decided to write one myself.
It was not an easy chore.
In nonfiction all the information must be true.
After gathering facts about Dunbar from old
newspapers, magazines, and books written for adults,
I wrote the first draft. It still needed a lot of work.
I cut and added words and moved sentences around.
Each time I rewrote a chapter, I liked it better
and better. This is the process I used to write
my first book, and I still use it today.

In 1972 Fred's mother, Mom Bess, came to live with us. With two dogs, a cat, and a tank of fish, our family was complete. We all grew together in our house on Pershing Avenue — reading and storytelling and letting our imaginations run wild and free.

By 1980, I had been a teacher and a children's book editor. I had sold poems and stories to magazines and had a book published.
Now, Fred encouraged me to follow my dream and write full time. He even offered to help and joined me in 1981.

Fred and I make a good team. We have disagreements, but we are always able to work through our differences.

Fred enjoys researching.

I enjoy writing.

It's fun turning the facts Fred finds
into an interesting story.

We have written many books together,

and we have plans to write many more stories
to share with children.

Family members are part of our team, too.
My stepmother Mary Virginia
and Fred's brother, Moses,
help us with our many projects.

Our son Robert helps with the research
and has written his first book, *A Friend for King Amandou.*
His twin brother John keeps our electronic systems
up-to-date.

Fredrick, Jr. and I wrote a book together –
Black Diamond: The Story of the Negro Baseball Leagues.
It was a Coretta Scott King Honor Book for 1995.

Fiction is as much fun to write as nonfiction.
I never begin writing a story until I know
the beginning, the middle, and the ending.
Some ideas are in my head for months
before they ever get written. One of my writer friends
calls it "*noodling* a story," which is like *mental doodling*
or doodling with your mind.
Sometimes when I'm noodling, I imagine
I'm listening to my grandfather tell one of his tales.

He had such a special way of saying things.
I disremember ever seeing a fox . . ., said Flossie.
Be particular 'bout them eggs, said Big Mama.
I want my characters to use the same
colorful language of the rural South
that Daddy James used.

To achieve that, I begin by telling the story.
I am a storyteller and often dress up and tell stories
to school children. Telling a story helps me to
write it better.

I then tape the story and listen to the words
over and over to make sure they have the right sound.

I taped *Nettie Jo's Friends* for Scott Cook,
the illustrator, to listen to while he painted
the pictures for the book.

"Listening to Pat say the words helped me imagine
what Nettie Jo and her friends would look like,"
he says.

Art is the illustrator's job. Writing is my job.
I take my work very seriously. Most of the time it's fun.
No two days are ever the same.
But each one is as busy as the next.

Fred and I may visit a school, a hospital, or a library
in the morning.

I may spend the afternoon writing or answering e-mail
while Fred reads over a set of galleys.
We live in a townhouse in a suburb outside
St. Louis now. I may work there.

We use computers, a fax machine, CD-ROM, laser
printers, scanners, and a cordless and speaker telephone.
We also have hundreds of books. We use all this
equipment and our library to produce the books we write.

Sometimes Fred and I spend the day in the park
or at the lake. We may read or use our laptop computer.

It's fun noodling a story by the lake.

Did I ever tell you about the boy
who caught a million fish . . . more or less?

Can you imagine that?
If you can, then you're well on your way
to becoming a writer. If you really want to write,
start now. Use your imagination!
Your friend,

Patricia C. McKissack

Other Books by Patricia McKissack

African-American Inventors; African-American Scientists;
Country Mouse and City Mouse; Messy Bessy's Garden

About the Photographer

Myles Pinkney is a freelance
photographer. He started taking photos
when he was twelve. He took photos for
the photo club in middle school, for the
yearbook in high school, and for his
college newspaper. Myles loves
photographing people, especially
children. His wife Sandi helps him a
great deal. They have three children: Leon, Charnell, and
Rashad. His children are often the subjects of his photography.

Acknowledgments

Photographs on pages 4, 5, 6, 7, 9, 11, 13, 14[top], 15, 17, 18, 23, 24, and 26
appear courtesy of Patricia McKissack. Illustration on page 10 [top] and
illustration on page 25 from *Flossie and the Fox* by Patricia C. McKissack,
pictures by Rachel Isadora. Copyright 1986 by Rachel Isadora, pictures used
by permission of Dial Books for Young Readers, a division of Penguin Books
USA Inc. Illustration on page 10 [bottom] from *Mirandy and Brother Wind* by
Patricia McKissack, illustrated by Jerry Pinkney. Text copyright 1988 by
Patricia McKissack. Illustrations copyright 1988 by Jerry Pinkney. Reprinted
by permission of Alfred A. Knopf, Inc. Illustration on page 12 from *The Dark
Thirty* by Patricia McKissack, illustrated by Brian Pinkney. Text copyright
1992 by Patricia McKissack. Illustrations copyright 1992 by Brian Pinkney.
Reprinted by permission of Alfred A. Knopf, Inc. Illustration on page 27
from *Nettie Jo's Friends* by Patricia McKissack, illustrated by Scott Cook.
Text copyright 1989 by Patricia McKissack. Illustrations copyright 1989 by
Scott Cook. Reprinted by permission of Alfred A. Knopf, Inc. Illustration
on page 31 from *A Million Fish... More or Less* by Patricia McKissack, illustrated
by Dena Schutzer. Text copyright 1992 by Patricia McKissack. Illustrations
copyright 1992 by Dena Schutzer. Reprinted by permission of Alfred A.
Knopf, Inc.

The classroom pictured on page 28 is the room where Patricia McKissack attended sixth grade at
the Robinson Elementary School in Kirkland, Missouri many years ago.